TOP TIPS:
ON WORING WITH
MIXED AGES

Maggie Barfield and Terry Clutterham

Copyright © Scripture Union 2010
First published 2010
ISBN 978 184427 542 7

Scripture Union England and Wales
207–209 Queensway, Bletchley,
Milton Keynes, MK2 2EB, England
Email: info@scriptureunion.org.uk
Website: www.scriptureunion.org.uk

Scripture Union Australia
Locked Bag 2, Central Coast Business
Centre, NSW 2252
Website: www.scriptureunion.org.au

Scripture Union USA
PO Box 987, Valley Forge, PA 19482
Website: www.scriptureunion.org

Bible quotations are taken from the
Contemporary English Version
© American Bible Society.
Anglicisations © British and Foreign
Bible Society 1996. Published by
HarperCollins Publishers and used
with permission.

The right of Maggie Barfield and Terry
Clutterham to be identified as authors
of this work has been asserted by
them in accordance with the
Copyright, Designs and Patents Act
1988.

British Library Cataloguing-in-
Publication Data: a catalogue record
of this book is available from the
British Library.

Printed and bound in Singapore by
Tien Wah Press Ltd

Logo, cover design, internal design:
www.splash-design.co.uk

Internal illustrations: Colin Smithson

Typesetting: Richard Jefferson, Author
and Publisher Services

Scripture Union is an
international Christian charity working
with churches in more than 130
countries, providing resources to bring
the good news about Jesus Christ to
children, young people and families
and to encourage them to develop
spiritually through the Bible and
prayer.

As well as our network of volunteers,
staff and associates who run holidays,
church-based events and school
Christian groups, we produce a wide
range of publications and support
those who use our resources through
training programmes.

CONTENTS

INTRODUCTION

In reality...
Like many churches, our rural congregation has a group of children aged from toddlers to young teens. We have one room on a Sunday morning for Sunday Club, and don't have the facilities, number of leaders, or enough children within any one standard age range to provide age-specific learning and activities.

There are many reasons why you might have a small group of children and young people with a wide age range – sometimes you might choose it, sometimes you may feel you've been landed with it! There's no simple solution to the difficulties you will encounter, no 'quick fix'. But there is more opportunity than you might think to build on the strong potential of this kind of group. It does have great possibilities, and can be exciting and rewarding when God cuts through the difficulties.

Why?

Before you read on, take a step back and ask yourself: 'Why have I got a mixed-age group?' That may sound a silly question, at first, but there are many answers.

Think about...
Not all groups of mixed ages are 'small' and not all are resource-poor. There are a significant number of churches where there are large numbers of children but few leaders so they have to meet together.

It may be that your church is small, with few families so there are few children. But it could be that you only have one space available in which to meet; or not many adults available to lead; or it was a conscious choice to meet all together; or it has 'just happened' that way.

Research by Scripture Union shows that there are at least six different types of children's groups of mixed ages. This *Top Tips* book is going to concentrate on the most frequent one and suggest ways to get the best from it. If you have a group with a handful of children and young people, with ages spanning from toddlers to mid-teens, with few leaders and often with limited space, money, equipment, facilities and other resources, this book is definitely for you. But, even if your mixed-ages group does not quite fit this category, you'll find ideas and hints here to encourage you and take some of the pressure away from this challenging task. Is working with a wide age range a blessing or a struggle for you? Or is it both? How do you feel about your ministry?

Let's be real. Most groups are a mix of blessing and struggle – and the struggles are significant.

> **Think about…**
> When Bear Grylls became Chief Scout in 2009, he said that there were 33,000 children waiting to join Scouts – but no adults to lead them (http://news.bbc.co.uk/1/hi/uk/8054699.stm). So this isn't just a problem for churches.

> **In reality…**
> I want to say it's a blessing because, well, because it is, really. And I should be happy that these few children are in church at all. But I dread Sunday mornings and I'm so relieved when the group's over. It shouldn't be like that, should it?

So, why is it often such a struggle?

- The children are spread across the whole spectrum of developmental stages and therefore have lots of different needs.

> **In reality…**
> It is not possible to sit and chat, in a cold skittle alley.

- There is a difference in body bulk and abilities; they are different sizes!
- Different age groups have very different interests.
- They have different levels of understanding.
- They have different opinions on music or worship.
- There may be an intolerance of the younger children by the older children – or they may well be intolerant of each other.
- They know different things: one may not have started nursery while another may be sitting major public examinations.
- They may be at very different places in their spiritual lives: young children may express their faith in God and their love for Jesus easily and openly; an older child may be working through complex questions of faith and doubt – and may also express their beliefs easily and openly yet mean something quite different from a 5-year-old.

> **In reality…**
> 'Our group was totally disrupted by one child' (with ADHD). Today five out of seven children have special needs…

- The leaders may be tired, feel besieged by the difficulties of the situation, be unsure what to do or how to do it, or feel unsupported by others in the church.

Which of these 'struggles' do you recognise?

Is there anything you want to add to the list?

Yes, the struggles are significant, but the blessings are also significant. God has put you in this place, at this time, with this group. Read on and look out for the blessings…

In reality…

An eavesdropping … 6-year-old: 'I'm going to be a Christian when I grow up.' 4-year-old sibling (after due thought): 'I'm going to be a giraffe!'

In reality…

My church is in the inner city. We get six to eight children along, with an age span of 2 to 15, including one with special needs and usually several children of asylum seekers. With a fluid community, I feel the odds are stacked against us – we are in downward-spiral territory.

1

PART ONE – BIBLE HELP

Let's be honest – there are no Bible verses that tell us specifically how to lead a mixed-age group. This kind of context simply doesn't feature in the Bible. We do have hints and clues though that our work with this kind of group can be good and can bear fruit.

God-followers together

Imagine the crowds of families of God-followers who for centuries, several times a year, headed for 'the place where the Lord chooses to be worshipped' (Deuteronomy 16:2,6,11,15,16), to celebrate the great Jewish festivals. For instance:

'After you have finished the grain harvest and the grape harvest, take your sons and daughters and all your servants to the place where the LORD chooses to be worshipped. Celebrate the Festival of Shelters for seven days. Also invite the poor, including Levites, foreigners, orphans and widows' (Deuteronomy 16:13–15).

Think about...

To what extent does the following description ring true for your group? 'At times the children and adults will walk along together, talking as they go, sharing stories with first one person and then another, each observing different things and sharing their discoveries. At times the children will lag behind and some of the adults will have to wait for them and urge them on. Sometimes the smallest children may ask to be carried. At other times, though, the children will dash ahead making new discoveries and may, perhaps, pull the adults along to see what they have found' (*Children in the Way*, Church House Publishing, 1988).

They all travelled together – toddlers, children, youth, adults and old people – to worship the Lord. This helps us understand how, one Passover, Jesus came to be 'left behind' in Jerusalem, his parents not being sure who he might be travelling with (Luke 2:41–52).

The family model

Bringing up children and young people in the faith was the task of parents supported by the broader faith community (Deuteronomy 6:1–9), and this happened all through the year. This was the best approach, according to God.

In New Testament times all ages met together for worship and learning, usually in homes – there's no suggestion that this was a poor second-best approach either. Children, youth and adults grew in faith by hearing the same things and sharing the same experiences. It was only in the early 1800s that churches decided they could handle things better if children and young people were split into age-specific groups – that they could learn faith in the same way that they learnt maths at school! Was this a serious mistake?

Of course God knew how best to nurture faith in children and young people – the emphasis was on families remembering, doing, modelling and learning together. For our mixed-age group, as leaders we're providing help for our group members to grow in faith either because Christian parents need our support in this or because our group members don't have Christian parents. As we work *in loco parentis*, there's no reason why this shouldn't be a great context for the children and young people to get to know God and grow in him.

Shepherds of God's flock

'The life of a shepherd could be very hard and lonely, as Jacob discovered (Genesis 31:40,41). Out in the hills in all kinds of weather, he watched over his sheep, leading them to good pasture, rescuing them from dangerous places, and protecting them from wild animals. Without their shepherd, the sheep were helpless. A good shepherd took his work very seriously; he would risk his life for the sheep if necessary (John 10:11), and would search for even one missing sheep until he found it.' (*The Book of Bible Knowledge*, Scripture Union, 1982)

Whilst we can't discover directly from the Bible how to run a mixed-age group, we can find plenty of help with knowing the kind of leader we should be. Let's explore 1 Peter 5 together, verses 2 to 11 which start with the image of Middle Eastern shepherds (verse 2).

Pause to pray for the 'sheep' in your care, and your 'shepherding' of them.

Remember that the 'flock' is God's, not ours. Our job is to look after it for him. We should be 'shepherds' who: do the job in order to please God, not because we feel we have to – it should be a joy (verse 2b); don't do it for what we can get out of it, but for what we can put into it (verse 2b); are models to our group of what it means to serve God (verse 3); will be richly rewarded for what we do (verse 4).

Think about...

Study these Bible verses with your other leader(s). What can you learn from verses 5 to 11 about yourselves as leaders of your group?

PART TWO – PRINCIPLES AND POSITIVES

2

For any church-based children or young people's groups, there are appropriate standards of safety and childcare that need to be met, including minimal staffing levels of at least two adult leaders (find out more at http://www.ccpas.co.uk). Ideally, there will be a pleasant, comfortable venue, and the church will be actively supporting the work of children's leaders. These 'environmental' issues are vital, but so is what you actually *do* when your group gets together.

Get to know each child well

The thing is, with only a few children, you can do this! You will spend more time with each child so you will discover more about their personality and their preferences. It becomes easier to remember who has the pet rabbit and who is learning to play the drums. You can learn about their strengths and weaknesses, helping them to build and develop the former, and overcome the latter. You can know them as individuals and about their family situations.

A small group gives you opportunities for great relationships between the leaders and the children and young people; and between the group members themselves. Other members of the church can easily get to know them by name too, so they feel – and are – part of the wider fellowship.

> **In reality...**
> Josh hero-worships Alex, who is 10 years older than him. One morning, they were sitting next to each other and Josh leaned over and said, in a very loud whisper, 'I wish you were my brother.' Alex is still smiling!

Think and plan 'family', not 'class'

Focus more on how group members can all help each other and work together, than on the difficulties with providing for each of them individually.

Children have little experience of being in a 'class' of mixed ages. At school, at Scouts, in sports teams and most clubs they mix with others of their own age. So it's not surprising if they find it awkward when they are in a church group with people of different ages, whom they only meet once a week, or less frequently.

But a 'family' structure is far more varied. If you think about a family sitting round a table and making pictures, they could all be painting, say, a flower, but all their pictures would turn out differently. Not right or wrong – just different, because the people making the pictures are different, they have different skills, and different ways of perceiving what a 'flower' looks like.

This can be the same with your small group: you can do the same activity or hear the same story, but the outcome will be different because the people are different. Not right or wrong; not too young or too old – just different.

Make any time with them fun and good

Just because the group is small in number, it doesn't mean you should only put in a small amount of effort! Make sure that the few you do have, know that they're welcome and that you're pleased they have come.

Programmes and sessions for a few children can be exciting and varied. There are things you can do with a small group which are much harder with a large group, like cooking or going out for a walk or watching a laptop computer screen.

The children can more easily contribute individually – they're not lost in a crowd – and you have more time to acknowledge them and make them feel valued.

Spot the 'God-moments'

Have you ever had one of those wonderful times when a child asks you, 'Can I be a friend of Jesus?' and, just at that moment, Callum is thumping George or it's time to clear up? With fewer children, you're not so distracted and it's easier to spot the 'God-moments' when they occur. It means you're alert to great faith-sharing openings and, because you know the children well, you will know how best to help them take their next step of faith.

Structure gives security

As leaders, you can feel more secure when you have a structure to your session. It may hardly seem worth the effort for a small group or perhaps the word 'structure' sounds inflexible. But a planned programme that is going to work for you and your group can free you to spend time building relationships and nurturing the children's faith, rather than worrying about filling the time or what needs to happen next. There's more about this in Part Three (page 20).

In reality…
If I've planned what I'm going to do, it's easy to adjust to what happens on the day. But if I haven't got a plan, I'm all over the place and everything goes downhill.

Encourage the older children and the younger ones

It's very tempting – and very easy – with a small group and a wide age range to simply pitch everything in the middle. But if you think back to the idea of the group as a 'family' rather than a 'class', that would be like everyone having to always do, eat and watch what the 8-year-old wants!

Encourage the older children to help you set up and run the group, and to mentor the younger ones. This is not a skill that comes naturally to most young people but, in the context of a small group, you have time to train the older children in coaching the younger ones. It's a good environment in which to build confidence – the older child leading the younger; the younger trusting the older ones. But…

Have activities that respect older children

Older children and young people are not spare helpers! They are not there just to help out or make your task easier. Make sure they have activities that respect their age and which enable them to grow in faith too.

But at the same time, you can help them to take real responsibility. You have time to take a risk on them and demonstrate your trust in them. Ask them to prepare the prayers for next time; or to book the projector and get it set up.

Give them real tasks to do that will challenge and stretch them – and be ready to pick up the pieces and give them another chance, if necessary.

Be aware of the needs of the younger children

As you need at least two adults with the group, consider making one leader responsible for helping the younger children.

They are physically smaller and uncoordinated; their language and understanding is developing and they are still dependent on adults in many ways, so think about how they can be included, whilst taking account of their age and abilities. Choose games where they will not get squashed and art activities that allow the children to be expressive without needing a certain answer. When you're planning stories or drama, remember that they believe what they're told and take everything literally, so be careful and accurate.

Improve your surroundings

You may not have a choice about the room or environment you meet in, but think about how to make it more cosy and relaxed. A few colourful rugs or throws can soften bleak rooms. Extra lighting can brighten a small space. A large room can feel like an empty barn to five children, but you can make it more comfortable by zoning areas for particular types of activity. Allow space for everything… if you have space!

You may of course find you have *more* choice of where to meet, as a small group doesn't take up much space!

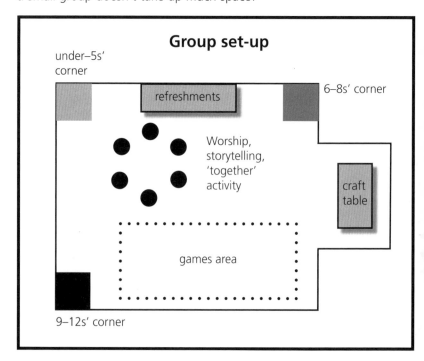

Be flexible with what you have

Where would be the ideal place for your group to meet? Look around the building where you meet: what is closest to your ideal? Can you use that space – or find somewhere similar?

Consider having age-appropriate corners in your space, if possible, especially for the youngest, with activities, books and toys for learning through play. Be realistic about a child's attention span and have enough variety and changes of activity to keep them interested, involved and occupied.

Think about how you can split the group into at least two age-specific huddles for some activities. About the age of eight, children go through a major development stage as they begin to understand moral questions of right and wrong, to begin to think in more abstract ways and have a clearer grasp of symbolism and language. So, depending on your topic, it may work well to divide around that age. Or you could group them according to their school patterns; or even try a boy/girl split for some of the time. Experiment and see what works well for you and your group.

It's easy to be disheartened about not having enough leaders, money, space, resources, time and support. Challenge yourself to:

- Work with what you have.
- Aim for improvement but don't focus on the future so much that you miss the present.
- Be specific in requests; target the right people and keep asking and praying.

Discipline appropriately

Use what you know about the children to recognise differences in ages and to encourage positive and appropriate behaviour. Every child develops at a different rate, though for most they go through similar stages of development.

In reality...
My son was very irritated on starting secondary school to find that more than half his homework involved colouring! OK – it was colouring in maps and graphs but to him it was 'colouring' and not what he thought he should be doing.

Children aren't necessarily naughty – they may just be incapable of what is being asked. Of course the opposite may also be true – they may be far more capable than we think and we may be asking them to do something that they find uninteresting or boring or silly because they are well beyond that level of development.

Create opportunities for the children to practise positive life skills such as sharing, helping and cooperation.

Use your knowledge of each group member to prevent difficult situations before they occur. If you can see a situation brewing, distract the child, intervene, negotiate – or change the situation so it can't occur. If Marcus is shy, don't make him join in until he feels comfortable, and make sure you include some quieter activities for all the group; if Molly can't read very well, give her something visual to help her; if Jack moans about everything your group does, try discussion and negotiation, and be more flexible.

Think about...

Look through the principles in Part Two (or read the 'Ten Top Tips' on page 29). Which do you think would have an impact on your situation?

Rank them in order, 1 to 10, for your own group.

Which is your Number One?

Start with that principle and begin to apply it, next time you meet. Don't try to change everything at once but get one idea established and then move on to another.

3 PART THREE – PRACTICAL IDEAS FOR RUNNING A GROUP

Part Two will help you think through the challenges and opportunities of working with a small group with a wide age range. Hopefully it has inspired you to treat this mixed-ages context as more of a blessing than a problem. But how can you make the best use of your time together?

What do you need in a programme?

Let's look at the basics.

You're meeting as a Christian group so the programme needs something about the Bible.

It's not enough to *know* the Bible: you long for children and young people to know God and develop their relationship with him. So the programme needs some kind of worship (remembering that 'worship' can encompass many different activities and is more than 'singing').

And it's all only theory unless you start applying what you're hearing, doing, knowing and being.

Think about...
Is your group-focus on worship, the Bible,
learning, sharing faith, building relationships
or outreach? Or something else?

So a programme for a small group with a wide age range needs to
include a minimum of:

* ONE Bible activity for everyone;
* ONE worship idea for everyone;
* ONE item to give everyone time to explore the Bible further and to
  apply it to their lives.

This will give you a strong start and you can, of course, expand the
activities beyond these essentials. How you decide what to put in each
of these categories depends on why you're running the group and
what you hope to achieve by the end of your group-time together.

In reality...
The hardest thing is to try and get a balance
over the ages, and it is the lower and upper
age limits that can get left out.

Session structures

There's no one solution – each group's context, composition and purpose are different. There may be different structures if your focus is, say, 'worship' than if your purpose is 'learning'.

Preparing a programme

It's difficult to plan sessions for this kind of group – their physical abilities and levels of understanding are very different, and you never know how many children you'll get and what age range you will have on the day. If a family with two children is on holiday, your group can shrink suddenly!

You won't be able to connect all the time with every child on every theme in every learning session. So don't get stressed trying! Choose material from the middle of the age range, assuming you have some children *in* that age range, and get ready to adapt it from what you know of your individual group members.

Think about...
What programme structure will work best for you and your group?

Here are three outline programmes, each with a different focus:

Example 1

A 'cell' group for 7–13s with a focus on building Christian community.
1 Welcome
   Icebreaker and snack.
2 Worship
   From CDs, or in more creative ways such as writing poems.
3 Word
   Bible teaching and application.
4 Witness/works
   Response to the Word in prayer or in a practical way.

This model helps build good relationships in the group, with plenty of group activities. The emphasis is on making an impact as God's people. It requires a lot of creativity, session by session, if it's not to become too predictable.

Example 2

A 'discipleship' group with a focus on meeting God through the Bible.
1 Settling and chatting time
   Setting the atmosphere, valuing each child, birthdays and news.
2 Bible
   Read or listened to, with visuals and possibly interaction.
3 'Together' activity
   Exploring the Bible further.
4 Response
   Prayer, praise, song, activity (together or in age groups).

This model encourages good understanding of the Bible, followed by a range of group or individual responses, as appropriate. The emphasis is on letting the Bible speak to

group members, individually and together. It depends on group members taking some responsibility for building their own relationship with God and with others in the group, and may have less of an 'entertainment factor'.

Example 3

An example from Margaret Withers, *Where two or three*, with a focus on worship.

1   Settle the children
    Invite them into 'worship'; introduce the theme.
2   Say sorry to God
    Silent prayer.
3   Connect with the theme
    Visual stimulus?
4   Read the Bible story
    Using illustrations.
5   'Together' activity
    Or open discussion (older group).

This model is like a mini church service, with the same kind of structure as all-age worship might have. This would provide a good introduction to more structured worship in church. Children who are used to church services may see this as a repeat of what they get elsewhere.

In reality...

There was a good response from children and leaders. Overall the session was lively and had an excellent atmosphere with everyone participating (if not always cooperating)!

Shaping a programme from printed resources

One of Scripture Union's key goals is to inspire and equip hard-pressed leaders like you! We provide a range of curriculum materials, *Light*, for different ages; *eye level* resources for holiday and midweek clubs; Bible guides; CDs and much more. See inside back cover and full list at www.scriptureunion.org.uk/shop.

But remember that any published material will still need some adaptation to fit your group precisely.

Think about…

What would need changing – and how? Decide which activities to use and which to leave out and why you've made those choices. How can you make the activities just right for *your* group? What's missing?

Knowing your group well will mean you're well-equipped to create appropriate programmes and group times. A publisher can provide you with raw material but you are the expert! You know your group better than anyone else, so be confident of applying what you know.

To shape a programme that is just right for your group, begin by listing the ages of the children. You may have a list that says: '3,6,8,14'. Look at the published resources available and choose a product that will give you a central core of material. Then adapt or tweak the ideas and activities for your group.

In this case, a good choice would be *Splash!* in the *Light* range. It is designed for children aged five to eight so will be suitable for the 6-year-old and the 8-year-old. You're likely to be able to find ideas that can be simplified for the younger child, maybe by reading aloud or substituting 'drawing' instead of 'writing'. Remember to 'respect the age and dignity' of the 14-year-old and adapt or add an activity that will help their faith to grow. (If there's nothing suitable in print, search the online resource www.lightlive.org. More about this on page 31.)

If you already have a printed resource, look at it now. (Or you can download free sample sessions of *Light* programmes for different ages at http://www.scriptureunion.org.uk/SU_Core/Light/TasterSessions/43375.id)

Determine what changes you would need to make before you could use it with your group. Ask yourself:

Is the main learning point accessible to all? (Check the Bible passage and the aim of the session: are the children in your group going to be able to understand this? Or how could you change it so that they do?)

Where is reading and writing involved? (Can this be done more simply, or changed to make it appropriate for the different age groups?)

Where might the physical differences between children be an issue? (Think about size, strength and speed. Can you play two versions of the game for different age groups? Or pair up a younger and older child as a mini-team?)

How much variety of activity is there, to suit group members who learn best through different approaches? Rhyme, story, visual, hands-on learning activity, repeated phrases?

Shaping a programme using *Mosaic*

LightLive (www.lightlive.org) is a revolutionary website from Scripture Union England and Wales. There really is nothing else like it! And it's free of charge (though donations are very welcome!).

When you visit *LightLive* you will find a special brand for small groups with a wide age range, called *Mosaic*.

Mosaic takes the hard work out of planning a programme. Each week, there's a mixed-ages session, chosen and compiled from the *Light* curriculum and following the regular *Light* syllabus.

Mosaic follows the principles outlined in this book so the programme gives you a regular pattern of six activities:

- one Bible-focused activity for the whole group
- one worship/response activity for everyone in the group
- two Bible-based and application activities for everyone in the group
- two further Bible-based and application activities to extend the session for younger children or older young people.

And:

- one page of visual ideas (which will vary: it could, for example, be a picture sequence of a Bible story, instructions for a craft activity, music for a song).

Plus:

- Bible background and preparation help for leaders
- recommendations from the *LightLive* activity bank.

It's easy to supplement your *Mosaic* session by using the search facility on *LightLive* to 'find an extra or alternative activity'. With more than 10,000 activities available, you need never be short of ideas.

A small group with a wide age range need not grow in number. But, with God's help and your committed leadership, it can grow in depth of understanding, in breadth of relationships, and heights of faith. Enjoy the blessings!

In reality...

A church in Kidderminster wrote to tell me that their children's group had increased by 400%. They were absolutely thrilled by the growth and success – and were hoping to get even more children soon. They had started with one child and now had four. For them, a small group was not a struggle or a failure: it was a delight and a reason for praise.

TEN TOP TIPS

1   Get to know each child well.

2   Think and plan 'family', not 'class'.

3   Make any time with them fun and good.

4   Structure gives security.

5   Encourage the older children and the younger ones.

6   Make sure the older children and young people have activities that respect their age and dignity.

7   Be aware of the needs of the younger children.

8   Improve your surroundings.

9   Be flexible with what you have.

10 Discipline appropriately.

RESOURCES

For small groups with a wide age range
LightLive new brand
Margaret Withers, *Where two or three*, Church House Publishing, 2004
ISBN 978 0 71514 028 4

More ideas from Scripture Union
LightLive as a digital resource
LightLive puts a multitude of Bible-based activities and ideas at your fingertips. Pick 'n' mix to suit you and your group. Take a bit here, take a bit there – compile your own session – print it out. Go to: www.scriptureunion.org.uk/lightlive

Light printed range
Exciting Bible-based resources for children's, youth and all-age ministry.
• Bible-based
• Fun and flexible
• Easy-to-use
• Published every three months

eye level holiday club and midweek club material:
Dave Godfrey *Rocky's Plaice*, 2010, ISBN 978 1 84427 390 4
Helen Franklin *Take Away*, 2010, ISBN 978 184427 502 1
For more information and other titles go to:
http://www.scriptureunion.org.uk/HolidayandMidweekClubs/2368.id

X:site events give children (7 to 11s) the opportunity to meet, worship and do God-things with large numbers of children.
Scripture Union runs holidays for individual children from 8 to 18s and for families, presenting the Christian message in thought-provoking and relevant ways. For more information go to: http://www.xsiteuk.org

Further help for leaders

Francis Bridger, *Children Finding Faith*, SU/CPAS, 2003, ISBN 978 185999 323 1

Ron Buckland, *Children and the Gospel*, SUA, 2001, ISBN 978 187679 413 2

Simon Barker and Steve Whyatt, *Top Tips on Leading Small Groups*, SU, 2009, ISBN 978 1 84427 388 1

Kathryn Copsey and Jean Elliott, *Top Tips on Communicating God in Non-Book Ways*, SU, 2008, ISBN 978 1 84427 329 4

Helen Franklin, Steve Hutchinson and Robert Willoughby, *Top Tips on Helping a Child Respond to Jesus*, SU, 2009, ISBN 978 1 84427 387 4